I'm Not Bad, I'm Just Mad

A Workbook to Help Kids Control Their Anger

LAWRENCE E. SHAPIRO, PH.D.
ZACH PELTA-HELLER
ANNA F. GREENWALD

Instant Help Books

A Division of New Harbinger Publications, Inc.

Publisher's Note

Distributed in Canada by Raincoast Books

Copyright © 2008 by Lawrence Shapiro, Ph.D., Zach Pelta-Heller, and Anna F. Greenwald
    Instant Help Books
    A Division of New Harbinger Publications, Inc.
    5674 Shattuck Avenue
    Oakland, CA 94609
    www.newharbinger.com

Cover design by Amy Shoup
Illustrations by Julie Olson
Interior photographs: Page 7 (bottom left) © Jose Manuel Gelpi Diaz | Dreamstime.
    Page 11 (middle) © Vadim Ponomarenko | Dreamstime
    Page 12 (top and bottom) © Monika Adamczyk | Dreamstime
    Page 103 (top) © Roman Belykh | Dreamstime
    Page 103 (bottom) © Dragan Trifunovic | Dreamstime

All photos are models used for illustrative purposes only.

Library of Congress Cataloging-in-Publication Data on file with publisher

14 13 12

15 14 13 12 11 10 9 8

Contents

A Note to Parents   **v**

Introduction for Kids   **vii**

Section I: Understanding Your Anger

Activity 1	There Are Different Kinds of Anger	**3**
Activity 2	Your Face Shows Your Anger	**7**
Activity 3	Your Body Tells When You Are Angry	**10**
Activity 4	You Have Anger Buttons	**14**
Activity 5	There Are Positive Ways to Express Anger	**17**
Activity 6	Understanding All Your Feelings	**21**
Activity 7	Reducing Stress in Your Life	**26**
Activity 8	Being Smart About TV and Video Games	**29**
Activity 9	Getting a Good Night's Rest	**32**
Activity 10	Eating Better	**35**

Section II: Managing Your Anger

Activity 11	Talking About Your Feelings	**41**
Activity 12	Using Deep Breathing to Calm Yourself	**44**
Activity 13	Relaxing Your Body	**47**
Activity 14	Managing Difficult Feelings	**49**
Activity 15	Taking a Positive Approach	**53**
Activity 16	Learning Positive Self-Talk	**56**
Activity 17	Developing Your Patience	**59**
Activity 18	Becoming a Good Problem Solver	**62**
Activity 19	Being Creative When You Are Stuck	**65**
Activity 20	Dealing with Being Annoyed	**68**
Activity 21	Thinking Before You Act	**71**
Activity 22	Handling Frustration	**75**
Activity 23	Keeping Track of Your Progress	**79**

Section III: Dealing with People

Activity 24 Taking Responsibility for Your Feelings   **85**

Activity 25 Seeing Other People's Points of View   **88**

Activity 26 Being a Good Listener   **91**

Activity 27 Getting Rid of Hurtful Words   **94**

Activity 28 Understanding Rules   **98**

Activity 29 Looking Friendly, Not Angry   **102**

Activity 30 Compromising   **106**

Activity 31 Being a Caring Person   **109**

Activity 32 Making Wrongs Right   **113**

Activity 33 Being a Good Sport   **116**

Activity 34 Holding Family Meetings   **120**

Activity 35 Cooperating with Others   **123**

Activity 36 Taming Your Need to Blame Others   **127**

Activity 37 Knowing What You Can and Can't Change   **130**

Activity 38 Using Humor   **133**

Activity 39 Forgiving and Forgetting   **136**

Activity 40 Are You Ready to Control Your Anger?   **139**

A Note to Parents

Many children today have problems with anger. In fact, researchers tell us that nearly 50 percent of all children referred for counseling have difficulty controlling their anger. Most often, this difficulty is not an isolated issue. Children with learning disorders, attention deficit disorder, Asperger syndrome, and other problems often also have difficulty managing their anger and expressing it appropriately.

The forty activities in this workbook can help children learn positive ways to manage their anger, using the same techniques they would learn with professional counselors. These techniques are based on the theory of emotional intelligence, which assumes that emotional, behavioral, and social skills can be learned in much the same way as sports, music, or academic skills. Once learned, these skills will not only improve your child's behavior at home, they will also help your child with friends and with the development of habits that lead to school and work success.

Each activity begins by highlighting the primary point. Next, there is a section that introduces a new emotional, behavioral, or social skill, followed by something for children to do, like a puzzle, a maze, a questionnaire to fill out, or a word search. Finally, there are follow-up questions for children to think about. They can answer these questions out loud, but it will be most helpful if they write down their responses (or you can write down their dictated answers).

While most of the activities can be done by children alone, they will be more effective when you or another adult provide guidance. You probably know from your own experience that changing one's behavior is not easy, and your support will definitely help.

You may find that it is difficult for your child to talk about certain issues. Never force a child who doesn't want to talk. The best way to get children to open up is to be a good role model. Talk about your thoughts, feelings, and experiences as they relate to each activity, stressing the positive ways that you cope with problems. Even if your child doesn't say a thing in response, your words will have an impact.

This workbook will provide a guide to help you help your child with anger, but there are other things you will need to do as well:

- Understand the reasons why your child is misbehaving.

- Have consistent rules and age-appropriate expectations for your child.

- Reward good behavior with praise or a point system.

- Be a good role model.

- Provide appropriate discipline for misbehavior, such as time-outs or taking away privileges.

This workbook was designed to help any child with anger problems, but your child may need some extra help as well. There are many reasons why children have difficulty with anger, and a thorough evaluation will help you pinpoint just what needs to be done. If you are concerned about your child's difficulty in controlling anger, we urge you to get help soon. Problems in anger management will affect many areas of your child's development, and you certainly want to act before things get worse. If your child needs professional help—or if you need some guidance—you will find this workbook to be of added benefit. Show it to your counselor, who may have some additional ideas on the best way to use it.

There is no wrong way to use this workbook as long as you remain patient and respectful of your child's feelings. We wish you success in the most important job in the world—being a good parent.

Sincerely,

The Authors

Introduction for Kids

Someone gave you this book because you are mad—a lot! Everyone gets mad some of the time, but some kids get mad more often than others. And everyone gets mad at certain things, but some kids get mad at many things.

But just because you are mad a lot of the time doesn't mean that you are bad. That's what the title of this book means. Kids (and some adults) who get angry a lot just need to learn ways to control their angry feelings and express those feelings in positive ways. Learning these things is like learning to do math or learning to spell or learning to play basketball. Being angry doesn't make you bad; it just means that you have to learn better ways to express your anger. We think this book can help!

There are forty activities in this book that will teach you many things about managing your feelings. You will learn how to ignore the things that bother you, how to cool down when you are feeling "hot," and how to get along better with kids and adults. We hope that you will find these activities fun. There are mazes, and word games, and puzzles to solve. There are stories to read and stories to write. Sometimes the activities and the questions may not seem like that much fun, but you should do them anyway.

The more that you think and talk about your anger, the better you will feel. We guarantee it.

Good luck and have fun!

The Authors

Section I   Understanding Your Anger

Lots of kids have trouble managing their anger. Did you know that you can learn to control your anger, just the way you learn other important things like reading, or math, or how to hit a baseball?

The activities in this section will teach you to recognize the things in your life that cause you to be angry and to understand how anger affects your body. You will also learn some important things you can do in your life so that you won't feel so angry. When you reduce your feelings of anger, you will find that it is much easier to enjoy your friends and your family. After all, it's fun being a kid!

There Are Different Kinds of Anger

For You to Know

There are many different kinds of anger. You may feel just a little irritated or you may feel like you have a violent storm inside you. You can learn to handle all kinds of anger and to act in appropriate ways.

Scientists tell us that we have more than three hundred different kinds of emotions. Some of these are "little" emotions. We feel them but they usually don't have a noticeable effect on our behavior. Can you think of some little emotions?

Other emotions are "big." When we feel these emotions, we definitely know it, and other people know it too. Can you think of some big emotions? If you need help remembering emotions that people might have, you can look at the list in Activity 6.

You may also feel one emotion, like anger, in different degrees. When you feel angry, you might be irritated, annoyed, or furious. Being irritated is a little emotion. Being furious is a big emotion. Being annoyed is somewhere in between.

There are different ways to react when you feel different types of anger. If you respond the same way to all the things that bother you, then people will just think of you as an angry kid and they will not understand what you need or want. That is what happened to Matthew.

> Matthew was a boy who seemed to always be mad about something. He got mad at his mother when she treated him like a baby. He got mad at his father because he worked too hard and was never home. He was mad at his teacher because he thought she had favorites in the class, and he wasn't one of them. He said, "Mrs. Friedman doesn't like me, so I don't like her."
> When Matthew was mad, he would scowl, fold his arms in front of him, and turn his back on the person he was mad at. When someone asked him what was wrong, Matthew wouldn't even turn around. After a while, people just stopped trying to talk to Matthew when he was mad. Then he was even more mad because it seemed to him like no one cared how he felt.

It is important to remember that there are different kinds of anger and that you can have different ways to react. Complete the sentences below to help you think about this idea.

One thing that irritates me is **annying people**
_____.

The best thing to do when I am irritated is **Calm down**
_____.

One thing that really annoys me is **when people talk when I'm talking**
_____.

When I'm annoyed, I can **punch a pillow**
_____.

One thing that makes me want to scream is ~~when people hurt~~ **when I loose a video**

Instead of screaming, I can **hit a pillow**
_____.

One thing that makes me want to kick the wall is _____
_____.

Instead of kicking the wall, I can _____
_____.

_____.

... And More to Do

Can you name five "little" emotions?

_____

_____

_____

_____

_____

How do you express each of these emotions?

_____

_____

_____

_____

_____

Can you name five "big" emotions?

_____

_____

_____

_____

_____

How do you express each of these emotions?

_____

_____

_____

_____

_____

What is one thing people do when they are furious that never helps?

_____

What is one thing you can do when you are furious that almost always helps?

_____

I'm Not Bad, I'm Just Mad

For You to Know

Feelings come from inside us, but we show them on the outside, particularly in the way our faces look. This is true of all our feelings, including anger. People can see that we are angry before we say even one word.

Take a look at the faces below. Can you see the difference in the angry faces?

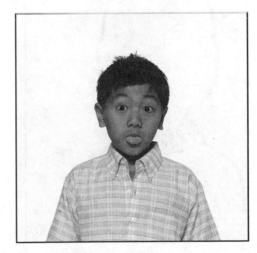

Now draw angry expressions in these four faces. Try to draw each one a little differently. Or if you'd rather, go through some old magazines and find pictures of people who look angry. Which face looks most angry? Which one looks least angry?

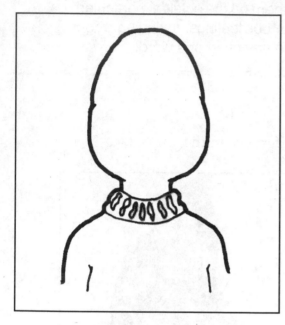
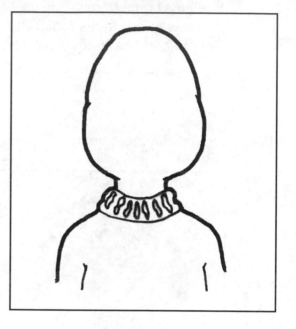
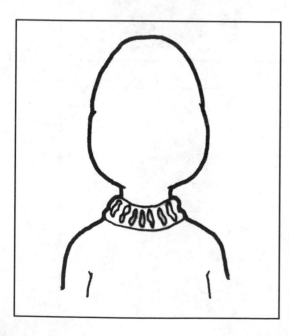
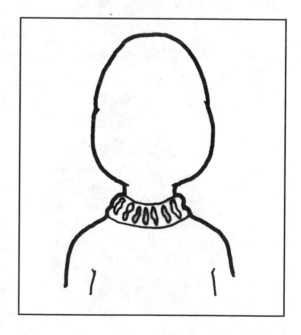

I'm Not Bad, I'm Just Mad

... And More to Do

Some people are really good at reading faces. What jobs would require people to be good at reading faces?

Animals have feelings too, and they show these feelings on their faces. Try to find five pictures of animals that seem to have different feelings.

Some people don't realize that others can "see" their feelings. Have you ever had someone know what you felt without your saying a word? Describe what happened.

Look through an old magazine and find faces that show these emotions: happiness, sadness, anger, pride. Cut out the faces and then show them to someone else. Ask that person to tell you what feeling each face is expressing. Are these the same feelings you thought of?

For You to Know

It is helpful to understand body language, because it is part of the way we express our emotions. Sometimes our facial expressions and our bodies say one thing, and our words say a completely different thing. When you can read body language, you will be better able to understand what people are feeling and you can respond in the best way.

When you feel a strong emotion, your body expresses your feelings. If you are angry, your muscles may get tense, your heart may beat faster, you may breathe faster and harder, and your face may feel warm. Sometimes anger may even cause you pain. You might get a headache or a stomachache if you are angry for a long time. Other people can see that you are angry, too, just by looking at your body.

- They can see you are angry by your posture (the way you stand).

- They can see you are angry by the way you hold your hands. When people are angry, they sometimes make fists or hide their hands in their pockets or behind their backs.

- They can see your anger in your face. (See Activity 2.)

- They can see you are angry by the way you position your body in relation to theirs. Angry people often step back from the person they are mad at to create more distance, but if they are looking for a physical fight, they step closer.

There isn't one change in your body language that tells people you are angry, but rather several different things that you may do all at once.

The pictures on the following page show kids with different feelings. Circle the pictures of the ones who look angry. Below each picture you have circled, write down the things about their body language that tells you they are angry.

... And More to Do

Have you ever walked away from someone who looked angry? What happened?

_____

_____

_____

Do you think that people treat you differently when you look angry?

_____

If someone looks angry all the time, what do you think will happen to that person's friendships?

_____

_____

_____

Suppose that you came home from school and your mother seemed angry, even though she didn't say that anything was wrong. Would you do anything differently?

_____

_____

_____

_____

Activity 4   You Have Anger Buttons

For You to Know

When you know your anger buttons—the things that set off your anger—you can learn to avoid them or cope with them better. You don't have to let people or situations "press" those buttons.

No one is angry all the time. There are usually certain situations or people that make us angry, and we can ignore most other things, even things we don't like. Everyone is different in what bothers them, but kids who have problems with their anger are usually more aware and more sensitive to certain things than other kids.

When there is something that makes us angry all the time, we call this an "anger button." It is like you have a little on/off button in your head, and when someone does one particular thing, that button turns your anger right on.

What kinds of things turn on your anger buttons? Check off all the things that almost always make you angry.

_____ Being teased

_____ Someone telling you what to do

_____ Certain noises

_____ Being looked at in a certain way

_____ Not getting what you want

_____ Unfair rules

_____ Certain schoolwork

_____ Certain chores

_____ Your brother or sister

_____ A certain girl

_____ A certain boy

_____ Something that regularly happens in school

List other things that always turn on your anger buttons:

_____   _____

_____   _____

_____   _____

_____   _____

_____   _____

To the left of the face below are five anger buttons. Below each button, write one thing that always turns your anger on. Below each button to the right of the face, write one thing that will turn that button off.

... *And More to Do*

Which anger buttons can you turn off by simply avoiding a situation?

_____

_____

Which anger buttons represent problems that you have to solve? Which problem will you solve first?

_____

_____

Does it help to talk about the things that make you angry? Who can you talk to?

_____

_____

Suppose that you had calm-down buttons instead of anger buttons. List five things that would instantly make you calm down.

_____

_____

_____

_____

_____

For You to Know

Everyone gets angry, but some people don't have good ways to express their anger. When you learn positive ways to express your anger, you won't get into trouble for misbehavior.

Sometimes you may feel like slamming doors, screaming, or kicking a wall. Doing these things won't help you feel less angry, and they will probably get you into trouble. Lots of people—kids and adults—have to learn how to manage their anger.

The game that follows will help you think about positive things you can do when you are angry. Here are some ideas:

- Talk about it.

- Draw a picture that expresses your feelings.

- Do something, like playing a sport or a game, that will take your mind off what is making you angry.

- Listen to music.

- Find something to laugh about.

- Walk around until you calm down.

- Take five deep breaths.

- Sit down and relax your muscles.

- Think of what is bothering you as a problem you can solve.

You will probably find that some things help you with your anger better than others.

The Cool-Down Game

Find a grown-up to play the Cool-Down Game with you. You will need a copy of the game sheet, ten pennies, and ten nickels. The object of the game is to get the highest number of points by pitching coins into the Cool-Down Circles. Here are the rules:

1. Each player gets ten coins, either all pennies or all nickels.

2. Take turns tossing a coin, trying to get it on a Cool-Down Circle. If it lands at least halfway in the circle, you can earn the number of points shown in that circle. To earn the points, you have to tell how you could use the technique in the circle when you are angry.

3. If the coin lands on an angry face, the number of points shown are taken away.

4. When all the coins have been tossed, the player with the most points is the winner.

... And More to Do

Write down five new positive things you can do when you feel angry. If it is hard for you to think of five things, ask other people what they do.

1. _____

_____

_____

2. _____

_____

_____

3. _____

_____

_____

4. _____

_____

_____

5. _____

_____

_____

For You to Know

This book is about helping you understand and control your anger, but you have lots and lots of other feelings, too. Every day you have feelings that come and go, and most of the time you don't even think about them.

Why do you think it is important to understand your feelings and the feelings of others? Circle the statements below that are true:

1. When I tell people how I feel, they will know me better.

2. When I tell people how I feel, I will feel better.

3. When I tell people how I feel, I will be more likely to get what I want and need.

4. When I tell people how I feel, they will probably ignore me.

5. When I understand the feelings of my friends, we will probably get along better.

6. When I understand the feelings of my parents and teachers, we will probably get along better.

7. If I talk about my feelings too much, no one will want to be with me.

The better you understand all your feelings, the better you will be able to understand and control your anger.

Understanding All Your Feelings

These faces show twenty different feelings. Next to each face, describe a time you remember having that feeling. Then go back and circle the three feelings you have most often.

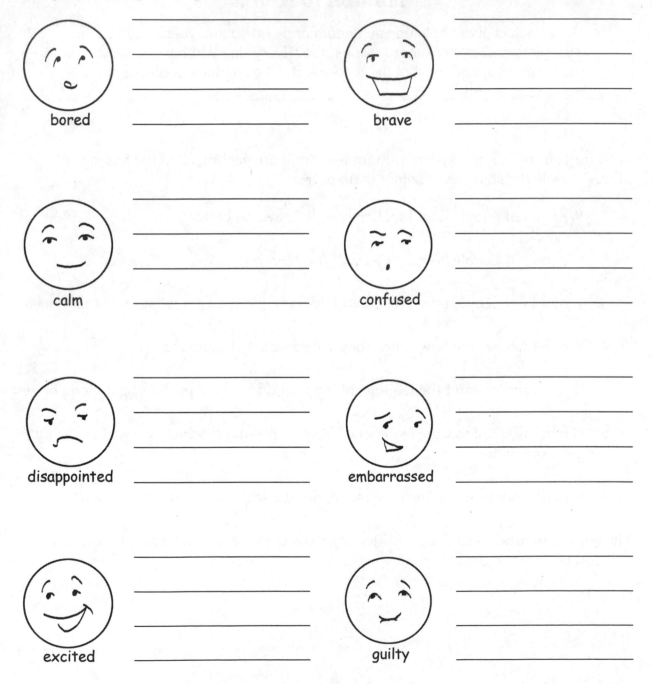

bored _____
_____
_____

brave _____
_____
_____

calm _____
_____
_____

confused _____
_____
_____

disappointed _____
_____
_____

embarrassed _____
_____
_____

excited _____
_____
_____

guilty _____
_____
_____

happy

irritable

jealous

lonely

loving

mad

proud

sad

A Workbook to Help Kids Control Their Anger

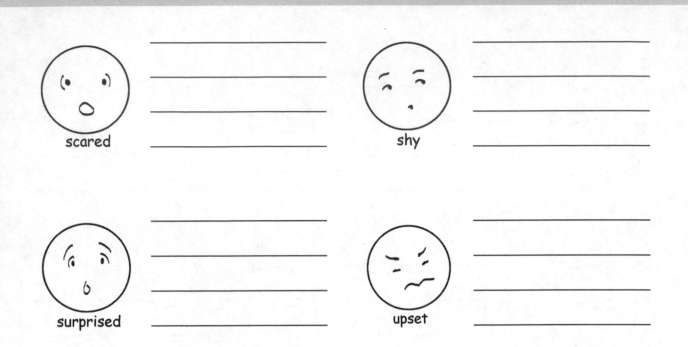

scared

shy

surprised

upset

... And More to Do

Did writing about any particular feeling bring up a memory you didn't like?

_____

Did writing about any particular feeling bring up a good memory?

_____

Why do you think it is important to talk about your feelings?

_____

_____

What three feelings did you circle as the ones you have most often? Was anger one of them?

_____

_____

_____

Go back and circle the feeling that you want to have most often. Now write down some things you can do to have this feeling more often.

_____

_____

_____

_____

Reducing Stress in Your Life

You Need to Know

Stress means that there is pressure on you that makes you unhappy. When you are under a lot of stress, it will be harder to control your anger. When you learn to reduce the stress in your life, you will feel better about yourself and others.

Too much homework can be a stress. Too many things to do in a day can cause you stress. Trying out for the baseball team can be a stress. You probably already know that these things can be stressful because they cause you to feel upset or worried or unhappy.

Even some things that people enjoy may be stressful, but it is often harder to recognize that kind of stress. For example:

- Some kids like loud music, but loud music causes stress to your body.

- Lots of kids like to watch TV and play video games, but too much of these activities causes stress to your body.

- Most kids like junk food and sweets, but food with a lot of fat and sugar causes your body stress.

- It's fun to stay up late, but when you don't get enough sleep, your body will be stressed.

When your body feels stress, lots of things can go wrong. Your blood pressure and heart rate can go up, you can get headaches or stomachaches, and you can be more irritable and unhappy. Too much stress can also make you angry. When you reduce the stress in your life, it will be easier for you to control your anger.

Many people go through their lives with lots of stress, and they don't realize that it is making them unhappy and unhealthy. You certainly can't eliminate all the stress from your life, and there are some kinds of stress that you just have to learn to live with. But even reducing stress just a little will help you feel better.

The following form will help you be a stress detective. You can use it to look at what things cause you stress and what can be done about them. You should complete this form with a grown-up who may know some stresses in your life that you aren't aware of.

Things That Cause You Stress	How You Can Reduce This Stress

... And More to Do

Having a healthy lifestyle will reduce your stress. Write down at least three things you can do to have a healthier lifestyle.

_____

_____

_____

What is one stress in your life that you can't change? Are you sure you can't change it? Can you do anything to reduce this stress even a little?

_____

_____

What are some jobs that come with a lot of stress? What happens to people who have these jobs?

_____

_____

Who do you know that can help you reduce the stress in your life? Tell what you can say to ask this person for help.

_____

_____

_____

For You to Know

Violent TV shows and video games make it harder for you to manage your anger. The less violence you see, the better.

Scientists have learned that if you watch a lot of violent shows and play a lot of violent games, you will tend to be angrier and more aggressive, even if you don't realize it.

Television has a powerful effect on people. Think of how many times you see commercials for fast-food restaurants on television. Do you know why you see so many of these commercials? Because the companies who own the restaurants want you to eat there. And guess what? Millions of people do—every day! They eat at these restaurants even though they know that many of the menu choices are not good for them.

But let's get back to violent TV shows and video games. These kind of shows may be fun to watch and these games may be fun to play, but they are not good for you, just like fast food is not good for you. There are plenty of TV shows and video games that would be much better for you to watch and play.

Here are six video screens to help you start thinking about what you are watching and playing. In each screen on the left, draw a scene from a TV show or video game that is not good for you. Write the name of the show or game under each screen.

In each screen on the right, draw a scene from a TV show or video game that it is okay for you to watch or play. Again, write the name of the show or game under each screen.

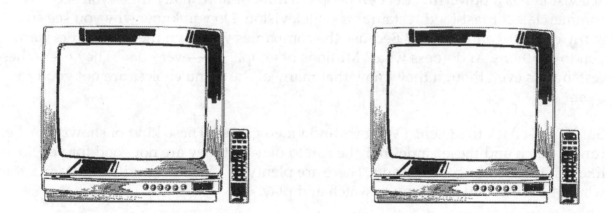

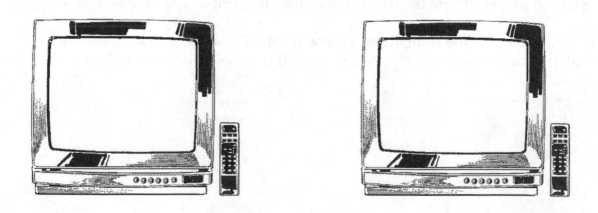

... And More to Do

Lots of kids like violent shows and video games, but they really aren't good for you to watch, particularly if you are learning to control your anger. What will help you give up watching these shows or playing these games?

Why do you think companies make violent TV shows and video games if they aren't good for kids?

_____

_____

Suppose you took all your violent video games and threw them in the trash. How would this make you feel? Can you do it?

_____

_____

_____

Suppose you could watch only one hour of TV a day. What would you watch? Why do you think it is a good idea to watch less TV?

_____

_____

_____

_____

For You to Know

When you get a good night's sleep, you will feel better. When you don't get enough sleep, you will be cranky and more likely to be angry.

Most people don't realize that sleep is very important to their health. Getting eight or nine hours of sleep is just as important as eating the right foods and getting enough exercise. About one in four people in the United States (kids and grown-ups, too) need more sleep. Can you tell if someone you know doesn't get enough sleep? Put a check mark next to the clues that tell you.

- ☐ They yawn a lot.

- ☐ They are grouchy.

- ☐ They have trouble paying attention.

- ☐ They are clumsy.

- ☐ They forget things.

- ☐ They complain about being tired.

- ☐ They lie around on the couch.

- ☐ They watch a lot of TV.

- ☐ They have dark circles under their eyes.

- ☐ They eat sugary foods or drink things with caffeine (like soda or coffee) to get energy.

- ☐ They don't do well in school or at work.

- ☐ They are forgetful.

- ☐ They have headaches.

If you checked all of these statements, you were right. They are all signs that a person is not getting enough sleep.

Some of the kids we know told us why they go to sleep late. Look at the sentences below and fill in the letters that complete each sentence to see why kids don't sleep as much as they should. Then put a check mark next to the sentences that describe things you do. The answers are at the bottom of this page.

1. I watch tel_ _ _ _ _ _ n until I fall asleep.

2. I like to talk on my _ _ _ l phone.

3. I listen to _ _ _ _ c.

4. I like to _ e_ _ my book in bed.

5. I w _ rr_ about all the things that happened during the day.

6. None of my friends know, but I'm afraid of the _ar_.

7. I like to stay up as late as my par _ _ _ s.

8. I like to IM and play on my c _ _ _ _ t _ _.

Can you list two other reasons why kids don't get enough sleep?

9. _____

10. _____

1. television; 2. cell; 3. music; 4. read; 5. worry; 6. dark; 7. parents; 8. computer.

... And More to Do

Do you think that you have the right bedtime? Would you be willing to go to bed earlier?

_____

_____

Having TVs and computers in your bedroom may be fun, but these things can also tempt you to stay awake. Do you have these in your room? Are there other things in your room that keep you awake?

_____

_____

Do you think your parents get enough sleep? How do you know? Do you think this is a problem?

_____

_____

How do you feel when you wake up in the morning? Do you feel energetic and in a good mood? Do you feel better when you get enough sleep?

_____

_____

_____

Eating Better

For You to Know

The things you eat affect your mood. When you eat foods with lots of sugar, you may get very hyper and have plenty of energy at first. But after a while, you are more likely to feel irritable and angry or even depressed.

Do you know the best foods to eat to feel really good about yourself? The answer is a balanced diet, consisting of protein (meat, chicken, fish, eggs), carbohydrates (breads, pasta, fruit, vegetables), and fats. There are fats in many different foods, including dairy products and meat, but not all fats are the same. Certain fats, called transfats, will clog your arteries and make it harder for your heart to work.

Eating a healthy diet means planning your meals and thinking about how food affects your body and your mind. Even though grown-ups usually buy the groceries and make most of the meals, you can still help yourself eat better. You can stop asking for foods that are not good for you, and you can try more foods that are good for you. You can also talk to your parents about family eating habits. When families improve their eating habits, everyone benefits.

Different foods affect your body in different ways. Draw a line to match the foods in the right column to the statements in on the left. The answers are at the bottom of the page.

1. This food has a chemical in it that may make you sleepy.   Salt

2. This food gives you instant energy.   Prunes

3. This food gives you long-term energy.   Water

4. This food keeps you from sweating.   Turkey

5. This food helps you build muscle.   Apples

6. This food helps you poop.   Pasta

7. Your body is made up mostly of this substance,   Steak
   and you need plenty of it each day.

1. turkey; 2. apples; 3. pasta; 4. salt; 5. steak; 6. prunes; 7. water

... And More to Do

Would you say that you eat a balanced diet? How could you improve your diet?

_____

_____

_____

Have you ever noticed that what you eat changes your mood? Can you think of a time when you ate too much sugar and got really hyper?

_____

_____

_____

What is one thing you should eat less of to be healthy?

_____

_____

What is one thing you need to eat more of to be healthy?

_____

_____

Section II　　　Managing Your Anger

Some kids see counselors who help them control their tempers and find better ways to express themselves. In this section you will learn the same techniques taught to kids by counselors, including deep breathing, positive thinking, and creative problem solving. The activities in this section will teach you how to control your emotions rather than letting them control you. All these techniques are easy to use, but just like any skill, practice makes perfect.

For You to Know

Kids express their anger in different ways. Some kids yell, slam doors, or talk back. Other kids won't talk about what is making them angry. Instead, they give people the silent treatment. Holding your anger inside and sulking never helps solve your problems. Talking about what is bothering you can be difficult, but it almost always helps.

Allen sulked and wouldn't say a thing when he was angry—which was a lot of the time. Once when his mother made him do his homework instead of going bike riding with a friend, Allen wouldn't talk to his family for a whole week! He wouldn't say hello to his parents in the morning or good night when he went to bed. He wouldn't say a word during dinner. When his parents asked him questions, Allen just ignored them.

In the past, Allen's parents had given in to his silence. They had tried to make him laugh, begged him to tell them what was wrong, and even given him toys and treats to get him to talk. But Allen still gave his parents the silent treatment when he was angry, and they finally decided there was nothing they could do to make him talk until he was ready.

If you've ever acted like Allen, this activity may help you talk about what is bothering you, even when you don't feel like talking.

Think of a time when you were angry and fill in the blank spaces below to tell about what happened. Then read this to someone who can help you with your anger. It may be the person you are angry at, or it may be someone else.

The thing that is bugging me is _____.
                                             (describe what happened)

When _____ said _____,
        (person's name)   (what that person really said)

then I felt _____ and I also felt _____.
        (your main emotion)   (a different emotion)

I know that I _____,
                     (what you did)

but that is because I _____.
                  (the reason you acted that way)

If I could do this all over again, the other person would say

_____.
         (what you'd rather have the person say)

Then I would feel _____
                 (the feeling you would likely have)

and then I would_____.
                  (what you would do)

That would be a great change!

... And More to Do

Has anyone ever given you the silent treatment? What did you do to get that person to tell you what was wrong?

_____

_____

_____

Why do you think it is hard for some people to talk about their feelings?

_____

_____

_____

Name two grown-ups you find it easy to talk to about your feelings. What is it about these people that makes them easy to talk to?

_____

_____

_____

Name two kids you find it easy to talk to about your feelings. What is it about these people that makes them easy to talk to?

_____

_____

_____

Activity 12   Using Deep Breathing to Calm Yourself

For You to Know

Deep breathing is one of the important ways for you to calm down when you are angry, worried, or afraid. It almost always will make you feel better.

Deep breathing brings more oxygen to your brain. It slows down your heart and lowers your blood pressure. These changes in your body all make you feel more peaceful and less angry.

Just taking slow, deep breaths will help, but there are also some specific ways to breathe that will make you feel even more relaxed.

- Sit in a comfortable chair and lean back.

- Pay attention to your breathing as you take air in and then let it out.

- Try to breathe from your diaphragm, which is the muscle in your belly area.

- As you breathe, think of a peaceful, calming place.

- Imagine that you are in this peaceful place. You can close your eyes if you want to.

Of course if you are angry at someone who is teasing you or yelling at you, you won't be able to say, "Wait a minute" and then sit down to practice your breathing. Instead, just start paying attention to breathing in and out slowly. If you have already practiced deep breathing in a comfortable chair at home, it will work much better when you are actually in a situation that is making you angry.

In the picture frame below, draw a peaceful picture that you can think about when you are practicing your deep breathing. You might want to draw clouds, a sunset, a field of flowers, or a boat floating in the water. If you prefer, you can cut out peaceful pictures from old magazines or find them on the Internet, print them, and paste them in the frame.

... And More to Do

Deep breathing works best when you practice it every day. When would be a good time for you to practice your breathing?

_____

Yoga is another way to learn relaxation and deep breathing. Do you know anyone who practices yoga? Are you interested in learning yoga?

_____

Relaxing is a good habit to get into, but that doesn't mean you will do it! Can you think of something that might prevent you from getting into this good habit?

_____

_____

Can you create a space in your home that will be comfortable for you to practice your relaxation exercises? What will it look like?

_____

_____

_____

_____

_____

_____

Relaxing Your Body

For You to Know

You will be most relaxed when you combine deep breathing with muscle relaxation. Doing these things together will help you learn to calm down when you are upset.

Learning to relax may seem like a funny thing to do. You might think that all you have to do is flop into a chair and turn on the TV and then you will be relaxed.

But we are talking about a different kind of relaxation. This kind of relaxation is for when you are in a bad mood or upset or worried. This kind of relaxation helps you wherever you are, and you won't need anything at all to make you feel calm and able to let go of your anger. This kind of relaxation helps you control your moods. When you learn to relax in this way, you can choose to change your mood, just as if you were changing the channel on the TV.

Muscle relaxation is easy to do.

- Sit down in a comfortable chair and begin your deep breathing.

- Beginning with your neck, try to relax your muscles. You can massage your neck with your hands, if you like.

- Now relax your shoulders. Remember to keep breathing deeply while you relax your shoulders and juts let your arms flop down.

- Next, relax the rest of your arms, from your upper arms to your lower arms, and even your fingers. Let all the tension go from your arms.

- Keep breathing deeply and relax the middle of your body. Relax your chest, your belly, and your hips. Let all the tension go from the middle of your body so that you feel like you are sinking softly into your chair.

- Finally, relax your legs. Begin by relaxing your thighs, then your knees, and then the lower part of your legs. Now relax your feet, all the way down to your toes.

- When every single muscle in your body is relaxed, continue your deep breathing for a few minutes. You can also shut your eyes and think about a peaceful place in your mind.

Relaxing your muscles takes practice. You may want to have an adult slowly read these steps to you while you practice.

... And More to Do

Lots of people feel tension in their neck, shoulders, and back. Some people feel it in their arms and legs. Which part of your body feels most tense when you angry or upset?

_____

_____

Do you often have headaches or stomachaches? Why do you think that some people have body aches when they are upset?

_____

_____

It is hard for some kids to relax their bodies. Why do you think this is? Is it hard for you?

_____

_____

Stretching also helps you relax your body. Do you stretch in the morning or before you exercise? How do you stretch the different muscles in your body?

_____

_____

_____

For You to Know

We all have many different feelings, including some that are upsetting. When you learn to manage all your difficult feelings, life will be much easier.

Anger is not the only difficult feeling people have. Here are some other difficult feelings:

- Jealousy

- Greed

- Worry

- Grief

- Envy

- Disgust

- Fear

Can you think of other feelings that are unpleasant for you? Write them here:

_____

_____

_____

_____

Some situations will almost always bring up strong and difficult feelings, such as the following:

- A hard test

- A visit to the hospital

- Someone calling you names

- Seeing a dead animal in the road

Can you think of other situations that bring up strong and difficult feelings in you?

_____

_____

_____

_____

The scale on the next page will help you understand and get control of your difficult feelings. Make several copies and cut them out. You can even use them as bookmarks. When you have difficult feelings, put your finger on the face that shows how you feel. Then see if you can use some of these techniques to help you get control of your feelings: deep breathing, muscle relaxation, relaxing imagery, creativity, writing, reading, taking a walk, or thinking about caring for others.

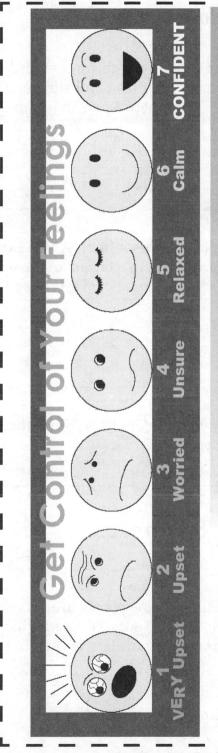

**Twelve Ways To Control
Your Difficult Emotions
(Anger, Anxiety, Fears, Depression)**

1. Take five deep breaths, letting each breath out very slowly.

2. Relax your body, starting with your neck and working down to your toes. You can massage each muscle group to help you relax.

3. Close your eyes and pretend that you are in a peaceful place. Use all your senses to experience this place.

4. Listen to quiet, relaxing music.

5. Stretch your body out like a cat waking up from a nap.

6. Slowly draw concentric circles. As you draw each circle, breathe deeply and feel yourself relax a little more.

7. Say, "I can do this," to yourself ten times. Each time you say it, feel calmer and more competent.

8. Read an article or a book about someone who inspires you.

9. Take a long walk, preferably in a scenic place.

10. Look at something beautiful, like a cloud or a flower, for at least five minutes. Pay attention to every detail.

11. Chew sugarless gum; it produces calming chemicals in your brain.

12. Think about, and be grateful for, all the wonderful things in your life.

Directions: The *Control Your Feelings Scale* can be used by anyone from age three to adult. Just point to the face that best describes your feeling. Try one of the above techniques for at least five minutes. Afterward, point to the face that then best describes your feelings, seeing if your score has risen. Try different techniques until you can raise your score to a 5, 6, or 7. For younger children, explain that they can control their feelings and feel better by using this special scale. Show them how to do any of the techniques by first doing it yourself.

... And More to Do

There are some people who have to conquer their strong feelings so that they can do their jobs. For example, soldiers have to conquer their fear, and surgeons can't allow blood to upset them. Can you think of other jobs where a person has to ignore a strong emotion?

_____

_____

Sometimes you can't ignore a strong emotion, and this is okay. A funeral is a place where people allow themselves to be very upset, but this is part of the way they say good-bye to a loved one. Can you think of another time when it is okay to express strong and difficult emotions?

_____

_____

Some strong emotions are happy ones. Can you think of three times that you were so happy you could have jumped for joy? Did you?

_____

_____

_____

Everyone has a different way to express feelings. Some people are very expressive and some are very quiet about their feelings. On a 1 to 10 scale (1 = very quiet and subtle, and 10 = very loud and obvious), how do you rate yourself in expressing your feelings?

_____

For You to Know

Some people always see the negative side of things, while others always see the positive side. People who are positive most of the time are usually happier than people who are negative most of the time.

Let's take a look at Ethan as he went through a pretty hard day.

When Ethan woke up, it was pouring rain, and he realized that he couldn't go swimming.

Ethan thought, "Now I can work that big jigsaw puzzle I started last week."

He took out the jigsaw puzzle and stared at the pieces. It was really hard.

He thought, "Maybe I'll call Mike and we can work on it together. That will be fun."

Mike came over, but when he took one look at the puzzle, he said, "I'm not doing that. It's way too hard."

Ethan was disappointed, but he said, "Let's work on it for ten minutes and see how it goes. If it's not fun, we can do something else."

As it turned out, Mike and Ethan really enjoyed working on the puzzle. It was a scene of a big rocket ship, and both Ethan and Mike loved to read and talk about exploring outer space. Then Mike said, "I'm going to be an astronaut when I grow up, but I think you'll be too short. They won't let you be an astronaut if you are too short."

Ethan started to get angry at what Mike said, but he thought, "I don't even know if that is true. I'll look it up on the Internet or ask my dad later."

Ethan's positive way of thinking helped him with situations that could have made him frustrated and angry. This activity will help you think about the things that make you angry and ways that you can be more positive.

On the chart below, write five situations that really make you angry. Next to each, write a positive way to think about that problem.

Things That Make Me Angry	Positive Ways to Think About These Things

... *And More to Do*

Who is the most positive person you know? Give an example of what makes this person so positive.

_____

_____

_____

How can you remember to be more positive even if you are in a bad mood? Is there someone who can help you with this?

_____

_____

_____

Can you think of someone from history who was known to be positive even when facing big problems? What did that person do?

_____

_____

_____

Is there one situation that you can't be positive about? Is there anything you can do to make this situation better?

_____

_____

Activity 16   Learning Positive Self-Talk

For You to Know

When you are angry, there is a negative voice talking in your head. When you change your negative thoughts to more positive ones, you will feel better about yourself and others.

Everyone talks to themselves. This kind of talk is sometimes called an internal conversation, which means it's inside your head. Kids who have problems with their anger typically say negative things to themselves. This negative self-talk is an internal conversation that keeps them angry.

You don't have to keep saying negative things to yourself. It doesn't help you in any way, and it keeps you from solving your problems.

In this activity you will learn how to have positive self-talk by changing your negative thoughts into more positive ones. Positive thoughts are just another way to look at things. They are actually more realistic than negative thoughts, because negative thoughts are usually clouded with your angry feelings, which makes it hard for you to see things as they are.

Here are some examples where negative self-talk has been changed into positive self-talk:

I hate school because my teacher is mean.

School may not be my favorite activity, but I can find some things about it that are fun.

My parents are mean because they make me go to bed so early.

My parents have certain rules that I have to follow, but as I get older, the rules will change.

Kids make fun of me and think I'm weird.

I can find friends who will like me.

This activity will help you think about your own negative self-talk and change it into a more positive way of thinking. In the left column, write down five negative things you say to yourself. Then change these into positive statements.

Negative Self-Talk	Positive Self-Talk

... And More to Do

Do you know anyone who is very positive? What is being around this person like?

_____

_____

_____

Do you know anyone who is very negative? What is being around this person like?

_____

_____

_____

How can you remember to think more positively? Some people wear a rubber band around one wrist to remind them of the importance of positive self-talk. Would this help you?

_____

_____

_____

Write down three positive statements that you can say to yourself every morning.

_____

_____

_____

Developing Your Patience

For You to Know

You can learn to be more patient with yourself and others. When you practice patience, you will become less irritable and less likely to be angry.

Most kids, and many adults, find it hard to be patient. We live in a world where the things we want come faster and faster. We like fast computers. Fast Internet connections. Fast food. Lines that go fast.

Nobody likes to wait for things, so it must be human nature to want to have our needs met as quickly as possible. And when we don't get our needs met quickly, we often get irritated and sometimes even mad. But being patient helps us realize that we can't have everything we want as soon as we want it. Sometimes we have to wait a long time to get what we want. Sometimes we have to work hard to get what we want. Sometimes we have to wait and wait and wait some more, and we still don't get what we want.

Being patient helps us be happy and calm even when things are not going our way. It helps us understand that the world doesn't revolve around our needs, and that is an important life lesson.

Perhaps you have heard the expression: "Patience is a virtue." Do you know what that means? It means that patience is an important part of your character, like being honest, working hard, or being kind.

Would you call yourself a patient person? You might be more patient than you know. In this activity, you will think about things you have to be patient for, because they can't be rushed.

Look at the pictures below. Can you identify all the things you have to be patient for? The pictures have been disorted to make it a little harder. The answers are at the bottom of this page, but be patient and you'll figure them out!

_____

_____

_____

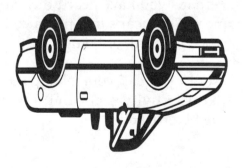

_____

_____

Answers:
Your birthday. Plants and flowers. Homemade cookies. Snow. Your driver's license.

I'm Not Bad, I'm Just Mad

... And More to Do

Most kids have to be patient while their parents are shopping. What can you do that will help you be patient during a shopping trip?

_____

_____

_____

Who do you know who is very patient? Give an example of how this person acts.

_____

_____

Learning a musical instrument, learning a new language, and getting good at a sport all take patience. Can you give an example of something you are learning that takes patience?

_____

_____

Tell about a time when you were impatient. What happened? What could you have done differently?

_____

_____

_____

For You to Know

When you learn to solve problems you have with other people, you will not feel so angry.

Kids who are good problem solvers don't usually have a problem with their anger. This doesn't mean that they never get angry; everyone gets angry some of the time. But when they are frustrated or when they are faced with a difficult situation, they think up solutions to the problem. When you realize that you can solve most problems, you will not get angry the way you may have when you were younger.

Children learn to problem solve by using these steps:

- Think of several different solutions to the problem that is causing you difficulty.

- Consider the pros and cons (pluses and minuses) of each solution.

- Try the solution that has the most pros.

- If it doesn't work as well as you thought it would, try to change it to make it work better, or try another solution. Keep trying until you have a good solution.

Learning to be a good problem solver takes some practice, and this activity will help. But the most important thing you can do differently is to change your attitude about the problems you face. When you decide that you can solve your problems rather than just getting angry about them, you will feel much better about yourself and about the people around you.

Look at the following situations and try to think of three different solutions for each problem. Then go back and circle the one that is most likely to work best. Talk over your answer with an adult and see if they agree with your choice.

Catherine and her sister Callie both wanted to be the first one to use the bathroom in the morning. Callie said that she was two years older, so she should get to go first. Catherine didn't think that was fair.

_____

_____

_____

Michael liked to play board games with his friend Paul. Paul usually got tired of playing after fifteen minutes and wanted to go bike riding. Neither boy wanted to do what the other one wanted.

_____

_____

_____

Mrs. Fried had scheduled a spelling test for Friday. The school concert was Thursday night, and the kids said they wouldn't have time to study. Mrs. Fried said that the spelling test had to be Friday, because she would be away the next week, and the class was going to have a substitute.

_____

_____

_____

Robert wanted to stay up until midnight on New Year's Eve. He said, "All my friends are staying up, and you're mean if you don't let me." Robert's father said, "We have to get up early the next day and drive to Grandma's house. If you stay up, you'll just be angry and cranky in the morning. I'm sorry but the answer is no."

_____

_____

_____

... And More to Do

Can you think of a problem in your family that needs a good solution? Think of three possible solutions.

_____

_____

_____

Can you think of a problem in your school that needs a good solution? Think of three possible solutions.

_____

_____

_____

Can you think of someone in history who was considered a good problem solver? What is that person famous for?

_____

_____

Can you think of some adult jobs that require good problem-solving skills? Do you know anyone who has these jobs?

_____

_____

Being Creative When You Are Stuck

For You to Know

There are many different ways to be creative, like painting, writing stories, or making up funny jokes. You can also be creative when you are stuck on a problem. Tapping in to your creativity can help you be a good problem solver.

Creative problem solvers find solutions that are not obvious or even always logical. One way they do this is by brainstorming. Brainstorming means thinking about many ways to do something, without thinking about whether these ideas are good or bad. For example, turn away from this book and think of all the different ways you could use a trash can. Then look back at the list below, and see if you have thought of some new ideas.

Here are some ways kids have said they could use a trash can:

- Turn it over and sit on it.

- Fill it with water and float stuff in it.

- Pee in it.

- Poop in it.

- Throw up in it.

- Use it to play basketball.

- Keep your toys in it.

- Roll it down a hill.

- Use it for a sink and wash your face.

Did you think of other ideas? Are you good at brainstorming? Remember that every idea doesn't have to be a good one. You can go back and look at your ideas later and decide which ones are really worth trying.

The boy below is thinking about a problem. In the thought balloon, draw a picture that represents this problem. Then in the space below, write down ten ways that he could solve the problem. They don't have to be good ways or even realistic ways. Just be creative.

_____

_____

_____

_____

_____

_____

_____

_____

... And More to Do

Who do you know who is a creative problem solver? What is that person's most creative solution?

_____

_____

Some people say that their dreams help them solve problems in a creative way. Have you ever had a dream about a problem that made you angry? What happened? Did your dream suggest a good solution to your problem?

_____

_____

_____

_____

Imagine you have a crystal ball and can look into the future. What does your life look like ten years from now? Be creative and positive in your thinking.

_____

_____

_____

_____

Activity 20

Dealing with Being Annoyed

For You to Know

When you learn to handle different kinds of annoyances, you will find it easier to control your anger.

Everyone has certain things and certain people that annoy them. Maybe it's your little brother or sister. Maybe it's the music your dad plays on the car radio. Maybe it's the way your friend brags about how good she is at video games. Maybe it's waiting for your mom while she tries on shoes.

While it is true that there are some annoying things you can't avoid, most of the time you can make annoying things a little better.

For example, you could try this:

If your little brother annoys you because he always wants to be with you,

you can spend just a little time with him and then do things that you want to in another room.

If your friend brags about how good she is at video games,

you can tell her that bragging is annoying you and ask her to stop. If she doesn't stop, consider spending more time with friends who don't brag.

If you are annoyed by how much time your mom takes when she is shopping,

you can bring a book or something to play with while you wait.

If doing your chores annoys you,

you can put on music to listen to while you do them.

If some kinds of homework annoy you,

you can reward yourself by doing something you really like after you finish your homework.

Draw a picture of yourself sitting in the driver's seat of the car below. Then think of five things that annoy you and draw one on each billboard. Look at the page carefully, and then put your pencil on the front of the car and shut your eyes! You get ten points if you can "drive" your car to the finish line.

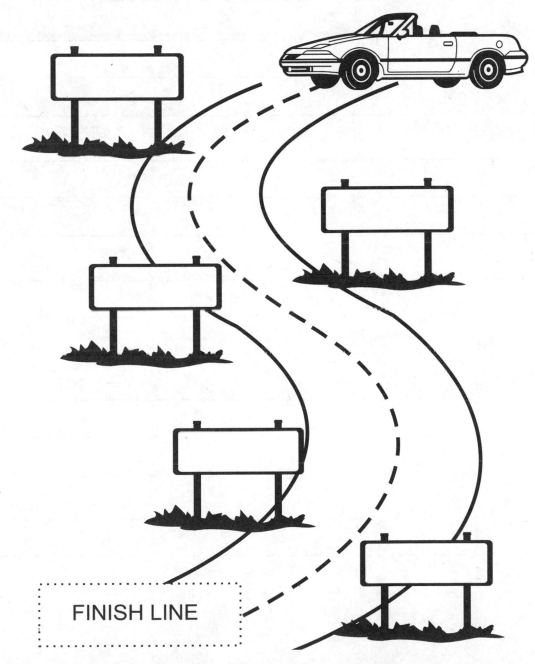

FINISH LINE

A Workbook to Help Kids Control Their Anger

... And More to Do

Write down the five annoying things that you drew on the billboards. For each, write what you could do to avoid that situation or at least make it less annoying.

1. _____

_____

_____

2. _____

_____

_____

3. _____

_____

_____

4. _____

_____

_____

5. _____

_____

_____

For You to Know

When you think things through, you can avoid many of the problems that are caused by your anger. When you learn to consider the consequences of your actions, you will act in ways that are more appropriate.

Adults sometimes ask questions like, "Didn't you think about what you were doing?" But the truth is that when we have a strong emotion like anger, we often don't really think—we just act. It is almost as if the strong emotion sets off a siren in our heads so that we can't think about the best thing to do.

Our brains are very complicated, and there are different areas that control our thoughts, feelings, and behavior. To keep things simple, we'll talk about just two: the thinking part and the feeling part. Sometimes both parts work closely together. When we have a feeling, our brains help us think about what to do with that feeling. But unfortunately the brain doesn't always work this way. Sometimes strong feelings, like anger, overwhelm the thinking part of the brain so that we just act without thinking about the best way to handle that feeling. That's why a lot of kids get into trouble.

The good news is that when we practice using the thinking part of our brains to handle our strong feelings, the feeling part gets quieter. It doesn't drown out our thoughts, so we can find better ways to handle our anger.

When you practice thinking about the consequences of your behavior, you will act in more positive ways that don't get you into trouble. Do you know what the word "consequence" means? A consequence is something that happens as a direct result of something you do.

Read the examples below, and circle the statements that are direct results of what someone did.

1. David went out in the rain without his umbrella and got soaked.

2. Sherry teased all the boys in her class. Eventually none of them would talk to her and some of them teased her back.

3. Sally was mad at her mother for picking her up late from school, so she got a D on her spelling test the next day.

4. Christopher hated to practice playing the violin. He told his mother that his baseball team kept losing because he always had to practice.

5. Veronica loved her red shoes even though they were a size too small. When she wore them, her feet really hurt.

Did you circle 1, 2, and 5? Those are the ones that tell about a direct consequence of a child's behavior. In example 3, Sally did not get a D on her spelling test because she was mad at her mother. She got a D either because she didn't study, or because the test was too hard, or both. In example 4, Christopher's baseball team didn't lose because he hated to practice the violin. There could be many reasons why they lost, but most likely, they just weren't as good as the other teams.

The more you understand the real consequences of your behavior, the better you will be able to control angry behavior that gets you into trouble. The following activity may help.

I'm Not Bad, I'm Just Mad

Fill in the blanks in the sentences below to help you think about the consequences of your behavior.

If I talk back to my teacher, my teacher will _____.

If I hit a friend in anger, my friend will _____.

If I don't listen when my parents say _____,

they will _____.

If I yell at my friends, they will _____.

If I act angry with the other players when I lose at a game, they will _____.

If I sulk when I am unhappy, then _____.

If I keep doing _____,

then _____.

If I don't _____ on time,

then _____.

If I'm not nicer to _____, then _____.

When I _____,

I will always feel _____.

... And More to Do

Are there some things you do that you keep getting punished for? Why do you keep doing these things?

_____

_____

_____

Sometimes even adults do things that they know have bad consequences, like smoking or driving too fast. Why do some people do things even though they know there are bad consequences?

_____

_____

There are consequences to misbehavior, but there are also consequences to good behavior. Can you think of something that will likely happen when you are caring and kind? Be specific.

_____

_____

Sometimes parents disagree on what the consequence should be when a child misbehaves. Does that ever happen to you? How does it make you feel?

_____

_____

_____

For You to Know

Anger often comes from frustration. When your needs or desires are not being met, you feel frustrated, which can make you angry. When you learn to cope better with frustration, you will be much less angry.

Frustration can come from different places, like in these examples:

Frustration can come when you don't get what you want.

Jenna wanted to be picked for the lead in the school play, but her friend Mary was picked instead.

Frustration can come when something is hard.

Shawn kept practicing and practicing his free throw, but he was still the worst on his team.

Frustration can come when you disappoint someone even though you tried hard.

Petra's parents said she could get a special treat if she got an A on her spelling quiz, but she only got a B.

Frustration comes when you disappoint yourself.

Sam wanted to lose weight, and he decided to stop drinking soda and eating ice cream. The rest of Sam's family had ice cream every night after dinner, and Sam found that he couldn't resist.

There are other things that frustrate many kids. Circle the ones that describe you. Then add any others you can think of.

I don't get enough sleep.

I eat too much sugar.

My parents bug me too much.

My friends bug me.

I put things off.

I spend too much time watching TV.

I'm in a bad mood a lot of the time.

I have an annoying brother or sister.

I don't have my own room.

Other things that add to my frustration are:

_____.

_____.

_____.

_____.

Some of the things that frustrate you can be changed or reduced, but others cannot. The best way to handle frustration is to learn to keep cool and not let it make you angry. Doing this maze may help. It doesn't look too hard for you to handle, does it? Well, try doing it using the hand you don't usually write with. Pay attention to how you handle your frustration. After you finish the maze, rate yourself, with 1 = I Lost My Cool and 10 = I Was Completely Cool and Calm.

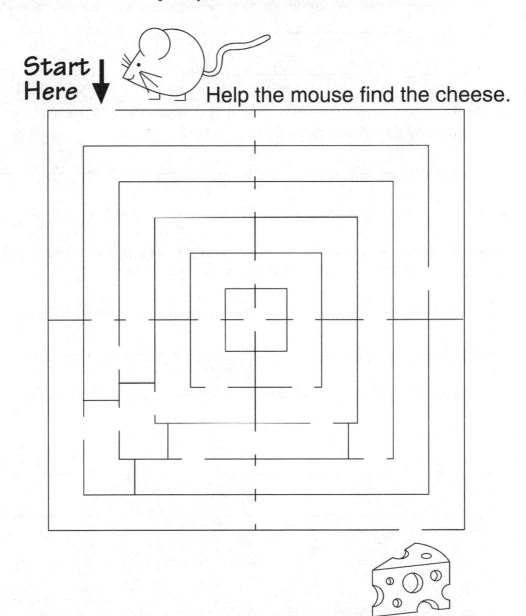

Start Here ↓

Help the mouse find the cheese.

... And More to Do

What is the most frustrating thing for you at school? Do you think you handle it well?

_____

_____

_____

Is there a time of day when you are more likely to get frustrated? What usually happens at that time of day that annoys you?

_____

_____

Is there a time of day when you are better able to keep your cool? What tasks, like chores or homework, would be easier for you at this time of day?

_____

_____

Do you know anyone who has a lot of frustration yet manages to keep cool?

_____

_____

_____

For You to Know

Lots of teachers and parents use points and rewards to get kids to try hard at things that are important. Getting points for good behavior is very helpful to most kids, and it is even more helpful when you self-monitor, or keep track of your own behavior. When you keep track of your success in changing yourself, you will find that learning new things is much easier.

Have you ever gotten a reward for something you did that was hard? Maybe your parents gave you a special treat for getting good grades. Maybe you were on a point system, where you earned points for certain behaviors, like controlling your anger or doing your chores. In this activity you will learn a simple way to judge how well you are controlling your temper. If you get a total score of 30 or more in one week, then you are doing a good job at controlling your anger—and you should get a reward!

In the space below, list five things you would like for a reward. Some examples are a special dessert, extra TV time, or seeing a movie. Show your list to your parents or teacher and see if they can agree with you on a reward you could get for controlling your anger.

Rewards I'd like for controlling my anger include:

1. _____

2. _____

3. _____

4. _____

5. _____

Make a copy of the cards on the next page and cut them out. You will use one each day of the week. At the end of the day, rate yourself based on how well you controlled your anger:

1 = I really lost it.

2 = I got a little mad but kept myself from really losing my temper.

3 = I did get a little mad and said some things I regret but I was pretty good.

4 = I kept my temper all day.

5 = I kept my temper and had a really positive attitude.

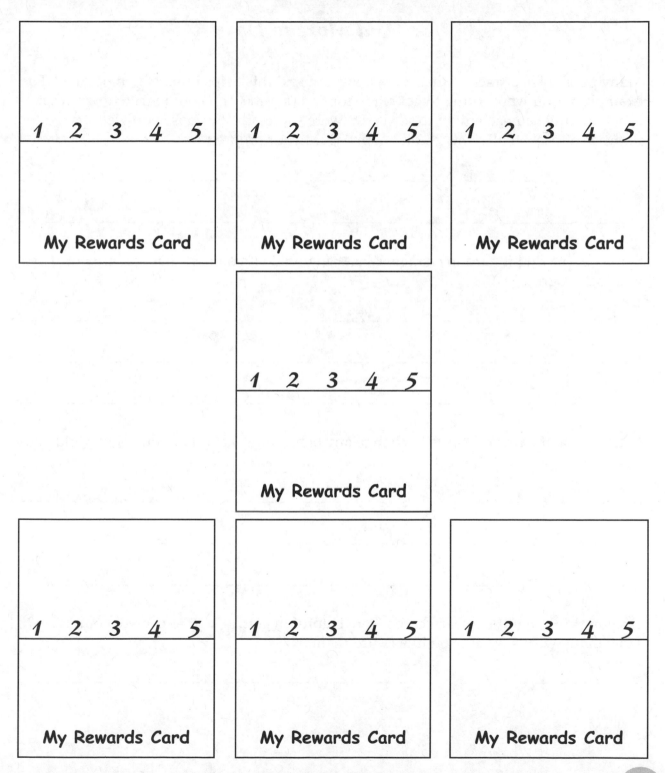

... And More to Do

Many people keep track of their own behavior, and this helps them stay motivated. For example, if you were trying to get ready for bed on time, you could write down what time you finished each night to see if you were successful. Suppose you were trying to improve at basketball. How could you measure your progress?

_____

_____

Some people find it hard to change. What can you do if you find that you are not making progress?

_____

_____

_____

You can use the reward cards to change any behavior. What other behavior would you like to change?

_____

_____

_____

Do you think that the reward cards were helpful in getting you to control your anger? How many weeks would you like to use them?

_____

Section III   Dealing with People

Kids who are angry all the time usually have problems with lots of people in their lives. These kids often get into trouble at school and can have a hard time making friends. They often get punished at home, losing privileges and special treats. That's not fun.

In this section, you'll find activities that will help you get along better with the important people in your life. You will learn how to understand people better, and how to act in ways that will make it easier to get along with just about everybody.

For You to Know

When you are clear about your needs and your feelings, it will be easier for people to understand you. Better communication skills will improve your relationships with kids and adults.

Many of us assume that people know what we are thinking and feeling, even though we haven't told them. One way to make sure that people understand a problem from your point of view is by using I-messages.

An I-message is a very specific way of communicating your feelings by filling in the blanks for the following sentences:

I feel _____ when you _____,

because _____

I need you to _____.

Here are some examples of I-messages from other kids:

> "I feel angry when you tell me I am not your best friend, because I really like to be with you and you are my best friend. I need you to not put me down."

> "I feel hurt when you punish me without giving me a chance to explain what happened, because I want you to understand the whole situation. I need you to let me tell you what happened."

> "I feel proud when you tell me that you think I'm smart, because I want to be smart. I need you to tell me that more often."

Do you get the idea? Can you see how this will help people understand you better? It doesn't mean that you will always get what you want, but it certainly will get you closer to getting your needs met.

Now practice by filling in the following I-messages for different people in your life.

For your mom

I feel _____ when you _____,

because _____

I need you to _____.

For your dad

I feel _____ when you _____,

because _____

I need you to _____.

For a friend

I feel _____ when you _____,

because _____

I need you to _____.

For a teacher

I feel _____ when you _____,

because _____

I need you to _____.

For a brother or sister

I feel _____ when you _____,

because _____

I need you to _____.

... And More to Do

Why do you think it is hard for people to talk about their feelings?

_____

_____

_____

What is something you need from your friends that you don't get often enough?

_____

_____

_____

What is something you need from your parents that you don't get often enough?

_____

_____

_____

Who is someone in your life, besides you, who would benefit from using I-messages?

_____

_____

_____

> ### For You to Know
>
> When you learn to see the point of view of other people, you won't feel so angry. Both kids and adults will appreciate you for being more understanding.

Very young children think that the whole world exists just to make them happy, but as we get older, we understand that everyone has their own feelings, ideas, and needs. We call this their point of view.

In our country, we believe that people are entitled to their point of view, as long as they don't take away rights from other people. This is not true in every country. Most Americans appreciate that we are free to have different points of view, and we respect the rights of others to see things differently.

A lot of times kids get angry when they can't see another person's point of view. You might not agree with a person but you can respect the person's right to see things differently than you do.

Here are some examples:

Haley was mad at her mother because she wouldn't buy her the sneakers she wanted. Her mother thought they were too expensive.

Haley stopped being angry when her mother explained that she had a lot of expenses that month, and she couldn't afford to spend extra money on clothes.

Emma teased her friend Julie about her new green glasses. She thought they made Julie look like a frog, so she called her Froggy.

Emma noticed that every time she called her Froggy, Julie didn't say anything but she looked upset. Emma realized that she wouldn't want anyone making fun of her either, even it was a joke, so she stopped calling Julie by this name.

Sometimes you have to try hard to see another person's point of view. When you are very angry, you think only about the person who is making you angry and not the reasons for what that person is doing.

This activity uses fairy tales to help you practice seeing another person's point of view. Fairy tales almost always have a hero and a villain. We usually root for the heroes and wait for the villains to get what they deserve. But every villain has a point of view, even if no one else in the story agrees with it.

Just for the fun of it, try to understand what some well-known villains might be thinking or feeling. This will give you practice in understanding that everyone has a different point of view, even if you think it is wrong. We'll start you off with some examples:

The Villain	**What This Villain Wanted**
The wolf in "The Three Little Pigs"	To have a good meal
A wicked stepsister in "Cinderella"	To be the prettiest
The giant in "Jack and the Beanstalk"	_____
The witch in "Hansel and Gretel"	_____
The wicked witch in *The Wizard of Oz*	_____
Voldemort in the *Harry Potter* series	_____

Now write down some people from history who had a point of view most others did not agree with at that time.

_____   _____

_____   _____

_____   _____

_____   _____

... And More to Do

Have you ever been punished and thought it was unfair? What was the point of view of the person who punished you?

_____

_____

_____

Do you know someone who is a different religion than you are? What are some of the things this person believes that you don't believe?

_____

_____

_____

What is a household rule that you don't think is fair? Why do your parents have that rule?

_____

_____

_____

What is a school rule that you don't like? Why do you think that rule was made?

_____

_____

_____

For You to Know

When you use good listening skills, you will be less likely to get into arguments. Being a good listener will help you understand what others are thinking and feeling.

The I-messages you learned to use in Activity 24 will help you communicate your thoughts, feelings, and needs. Now you need to learn to be a good listener.

Being a good listener takes some practice. Ask an adult to help you practice these three steps.

1. **Look at the person who is talking to you.**
   Most of the time you will look the person in the eyes, because this is a signal that you are paying attention. But you should also look at the person's facial expression and body language. Good communication is built on both looking and listening.

2. **Don't interrupt.**
   Even if you disagree with what the person is saying, and even if you have something important to say, don't interrupt. Good listening means completely understanding what another person is saying before you reply. Interrupting is rude and shows that you are not really serious about listening.

3. **Repeat what you hear.**
   This may seem a little weird the first time you do it, but it is easy to do. Just repeat what the person has told you, either in the same words or in a summary. Ask if you got it right. For example, you might say: "It sounds like you were mad at me because I didn't call you last night. Is that what you are saying?" It is important to say this in a calm tone of voice. If you have anger or sarcasm in your voice, that will just lead to an argument.

You may need to ask questions to really understand what a person is telling you. Again, make sure that you use a calm tone of voice and don't sound critical. Listen to the answers carefully without interrupting, and repeat what you hear.

When you are a good listener, you understand what a person is really saying, not just what you think they are saying. It's something like reading. When you read a book, you can't make sense of the story one word at a time. Instead, you have to think about what the whole book means.

See if you can read the paragraph below. It may be hard at first. Now cross out every k, q, and v. Then read the paragraph again.

Leakrniqng to livsten will khelp yoku with yoqur fvrieqnds andk with avdulqts, too. Whevn yoqu bekcomve a govvod listenqer, yovu wikll alsvo finqd thqavt peqopkle pkay vmore attvkention to yovu.

... And More to Do

Can you think of an adult job where it is important to be a good listener?

_____

_____

Who in your life is a good listener? Is this someone you like to talk to?

_____

_____

Think of a time when you were talking to someone and felt like that person wasn't listening to you. What happened?

_____

_____

_____

_____

Who is one person that needs to know you are now a good listener? What is something you need to talk about with this person?

_____

_____

_____

_____

For You to Know

You can learn to stop using words that make other people angry or hurt their feelings. There are ways to express your feelings without hurting others.

Everyone has certain words that make them angry. People usually get very angry if you use words that make fun of their race, religion, family, or ethnic background. Most people will get angry if you use words that make fun of their differences. For example, someone who is short won't like being called "Shorty" and someone who wears glasses won't like being called "Four-Eyes."

What are some words or phrases that always make you angry? Write them in the space below:

_____

_____

_____

_____

You might also use words that make people angry at you.

Write in words that you should never say to your parents. (If these are curse words, you shouldn't even write them. When people want to write a curse word, they just put the first letter of that word, followed by X's.)

_____

_____

_____

_____

_____

Write in words that you should never say in school.

_____

_____

_____

_____

_____

The Rip-Up Game can help you get rid of hurtful words. To play, make a copy of the next page. In each of the ten boxes, write hurtful words or phrases that will get you or someone else angry. (Remember that if you want to write a curse word, just put the first letter followed by X's.) Now cut out the cards and rip them up! See how many small pieces you can make.

If someone tries to make you mad with one of these words in the future, remember that you have ripped these words up, and they can no longer make you angry.

I'm Not Bad, I'm Just Mad

... And More to Do

Why do you think kids use hurtful words?

_____

_____

_____

Do adults ever say certain words that hurt your feelings? What can you say to tell them how you feel?

_____

_____

Sarcasm can also hurt people's feelings. When people are sarcastic, it is not the words themselves that are hurtful, but the way they are said. Can you tell about a time when someone was sarcastic to you?

_____

_____

_____

Sometimes jokes hurt people's feelings. Think of a joke that might be insulting. What would you say to someone who told this joke?

_____

_____

_____

Activity 28   Understanding Rules

For You to Know

All kids and adults have to live with rules. You probably accept most rules as just being part of life. But some rules may be harder for you to accept. Understanding the rules that affect you will help you see that there are things in your life you can change and things in your life that you can't change.

There are many different kinds of rules. Kids have rules about what they eat, when they do their homework, what their responsibilities are around the house, what they can and can't say, and many more things. Adults have rules, too. Adults have to pay their bills and taxes on time. They have to be at work on time and get their work done on time.

Some rules are laws. Laws are rules that everyone has to obey, such as:

- You have to obey traffic laws, whether you are driving, walking, or riding a bike.

- You can't steal.

- You can't smoke cigarettes or drink alcohol until you are twenty-one.

- You can't destroy public property.

- You can't litter.

Anyone who breaks these laws can get into serious trouble and may even go to jail.

Can you think of some more laws?

1. _____

2. _____

3. _____

Other rules tell us what is right and wrong. We call these moral rules. You won't go to jail if you break these rules, but you can get into trouble. If you break moral rules, people will certainly think less of you.

Some examples of moral rules are:

- Don't lie.

- Don't cheat.

- Don't make fun of people.

Can you think of some other moral rules?

1. _____

2. _____

3. _____

It is important to follow moral rules to get along with others. You will have a hard time in school or in your family if you don't follow moral rules.

There are also personal rules that guide our behavior. Everyone has personal rules or values that they try to follow. Some personal rules would include:

- Be kind to others.

- Be responsible and take care of your things.

- Be respectful to adults.

Can you think of some other personal rules that are important to you?

1. _____

2. _____

3. _____

Your personal rules tell a lot about the kind of person that you are. A person with good values will be liked and appreciated by many people.

Look at the five signs below. Write in five rules that you think are important for you to remember. They can be laws, moral rules, or personal rules.

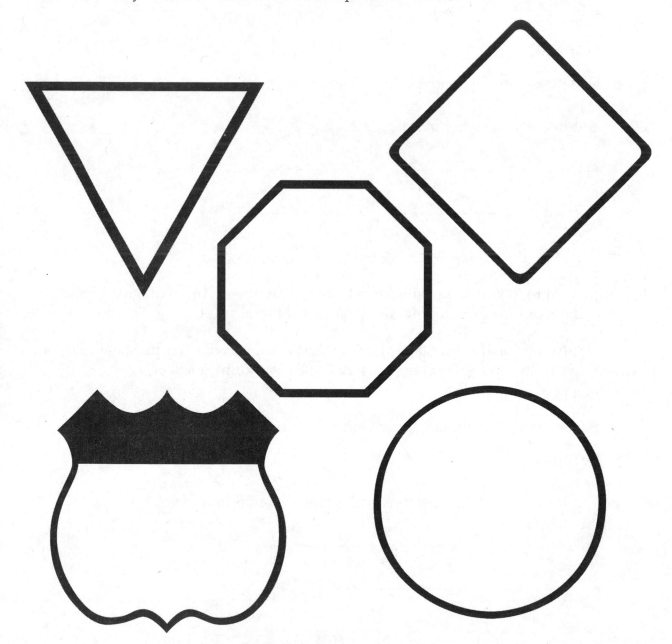

... And More to Do

Are there some rules at home that are harder for you to follow than others?

_____

_____

_____

Are there some rules at school that are harder for you to follow?

_____

_____

_____

If you think a rule is unfair, what is the best thing for you to do?

_____

_____

_____

Which personal rule is most important to you?

_____

_____

_____

> ## *For You to Know*
>
> If you look angry a lot of the time, it will be hard to make friends. It is hard to talk to people who look angry, and it is certainly hard to do fun things with someone who always looks angry.

Did you know that some people get in the habit of looking angry even when they are not? When you look angry, you usually frown. You might stare hard at people, you might cross your arms, and you might use other types of body language that puts people off.

Did you know that even teachers like kids better when they look friendly? Scientists tell us that teachers pay more attention to kids who look friendly and even give them better grades! When you look friendly, you smile. Your shoulders and body look relaxed, and sometimes there is even a twinkle in your eye.

In this activity, you will think about the kinds of things that make people look angry and the kinds of the things that make them look friendly.

Look at the two kids below. List all the things that make them look angry.

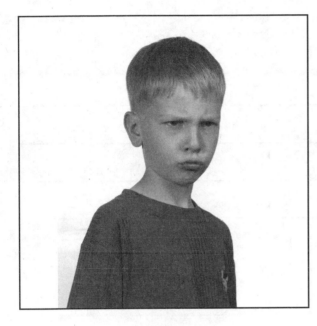

_____

_____

_____

_____

_____

_____

_____

_____

Now look at these two kids. List all the things that make them look friendly.

_____

_____

_____

_____

_____

_____

_____

_____

... And More to Do

Can you think of a time when it is really important for you to look friendly?

_____

_____

Can you think of a time when you thought someone was angry at you, but it turned out that they really weren't?

_____

_____

Can you think of three gestures that show that you are friendly?

_____

_____

_____

Do you think that just smiling at someone will make that person think you are friendly? Explain your answer.

_____

_____

_____

For You to Know

When you want something, instead of getting angry you can try to work out a compromise. A compromise is when two people agree to do something that will make each of them happy. When you learn to compromise, you will find fewer reasons to be angry.

A lot of times kids get angry when they don't get their way. They may think that getting angry will help them get what they want, but this is rarely true. Most of the time getting angry just makes things worse, as in the following examples:

- Mary fought with her sister over which TV show they would watch. Their father said that whenever they fight, no one will be able to watch TV for a week.

- Nate got mad at his mother because she yelled at him for not doing his homework. She decided that she wouldn't let him play video games until he showed that he could be more responsible.

- Brian sulked because he didn't want to go to his grandparents' house for dinner. His mother made him write an apology to his grandparents for his behavior.

Not every situation can be solved with a compromise. Sometimes kids just have to do what adults want, whether they like it or not. Then the best thing that kids can do is cooperate. Cooperating means doing something for someone else without complaining, just because it will help that person out.

Some kids are great compromisers. Whenever two people have a problem, they can think of a solution both can agree to. People usually get along well with great compromisers and like to have them around. These situations will help you practice working out compromises. In Activity 35, you will learn more about the importance of cooperating.

Shaina and her brother fought about what TV program to watch. What would you tell them to do?

_____

_____

_____

Keith wanted to stop taking piano lessons. His mother said that when he was grown up he would thank for her for making him take piano lessons. What compromise would you suggest?

_____

_____

_____

Sara wanted to eat only pasta for dinner. Her mother said that she had to eat some kind of protein and vegetables and fruit at every meal. But Sara only liked pasta! What would you suggest?

_____

_____

_____

Heather liked to sleep late on the weekends. Her mom wanted her to get up early on Saturdays to do her chores and on Sundays to go to Sunday school. Heather thought this was unfair. Can you think of a compromise for Heather and her mom?

_____

_____

_____

... *And More to Do*

Describe a good compromise that you made with someone.

_____

_____

_____

Describe a situation where you need to cooperate even though it may be hard to do.

_____

_____

_____

Why do you think it is important to be as cooperative as possible?

_____

_____

_____

What would happen if a group of people didn't want to cooperate or compromise? Have you ever heard of a situation like this?

_____

_____

_____

Being a Caring Person Activity 31

For You to Know

In earlier activities, you learned that you can change your angry feelings by positive thinking. You can also change your angry feelings by changing your behavior. The more you are kind and caring, the less you will be angry.

It is almost impossible to be angry when you are doing something that shows other people you care about them. But controlling your anger is not the reason that anyone becomes a caring person. Caring about others is a great way live in this world, the right way to be a human being.

Everyone likes kids who are kind, caring, and helpful. When you show that you care about people—your family, your friends, even strangers who need help because they are hungry or homeless—you will feel very good about yourself, and others will feel good about you, too! But do you know the most important reason that you should do good things for others? Read the story below to find out.

Darcy was the most helpful child anyone had ever known. Her teachers, her parents, her friends, and even the dogs and cats in the neighborhood knew that if they ever needed anything, Darcy would be there to help.

When Mrs. Fiddler, Darcy's teacher, lost her purse, Darcy looked all over the school and found it under a bush. (Don't ask how it got there. No one seemed to know.)

When Darcy's father came home from work with a headache, Darcy immediately turned off the TV, dimmed the living-room lights, and brought him a glass of cold water.

When Darcy's friend Damon was sick and had to go to the hospital for a week, Darcy visited or called every day. Damon always felt better when they talked.

When Darcy saw a stray cat or a lost dog, she immediately told her mother, and they both helped the animal. By last count, Darcy had returned seventeen pets to their owners and found new homes for three more.

The news of Darcy's helpfulness spread far and wide. People all over her state began to talk about Darcy and how much they admired her. Many children began trying to be more helpful. They formed Helping Clubs, and they

A Workbook to Help Kids Control Their Anger

wrote to Darcy for an autographed picture to hang on the wall. Darcy became the most popular name for new babies. Many parents said, "If we call our baby Darcy, perhaps she will grow up to be helpful like the real Darcy. Wouldn't that be wonderful!?"

Eventually, even the governor heard about Darcy's helpfulness. He decided to establish a special scientific committee to study Darcy to find out what made her so helpful. Darcy's parents said that this would be all right since they certainly wanted everyone to be more helpful. (And you are probably not surprised to hear that Darcy wanted to help people be more helpful!)

Six famous doctors came to Darcy's home and lived with her for a week. They followed her around and gave her a physical examination. They watched her eat and even watched her sleep. Every night they would gather to talk about what they had learned. And every night, they always ended up talking about all the helpful things Darcy had done that day. At the end of the week, the doctors wrote a report to submit to the governor. It didn't take them very much time, because it only had one sentence.

The Moral of the Story: Good deeds are their own reward.

Perhaps you are wondering how you can be like Darcy and show that you care about people. This word scramble will help you figure it out. See if you can unscramble these seven ways to show that you care about others. The solutions are at the bottom of the page.

olhd hte doro

asy I lvoe ouy

od xerta hocrse

noadte ot chyriat

ekep yuro omor clnea

ismle hwne oyu emet omnseoe

eb plotei nda sue ogdo smnaern

Answers:

Hold the door.

Say I love you.

Do extra chores.

Donate to charity.

Keep your room clean.

Smile when you meet someone.

Be polite and use good manners.

... *And More to Do*

There are many things kids do every day to show that they care. In the space below, see if you can list ten things that you can do. If you need help thinking of ways to show caring and kindness, there are two websites we recommend: www.kidscareclubs.org and www.actsofkindness.org.

1. _____

2. _____

3. _____

4. _____

5. _____

6. _____

7. _____

8. _____

9. _____

10. _____

Making Wrongs Right

> ## *For You to Know*
>
> When you do or say something in anger, it helps to apologize—if you really mean it. Sometimes kids just say, "I'm sorry," but they don't really mean it. Parents or friends might accept your apology, but people can tell when someone really means what they say.

Some kids find themselves apologizing over and over again for doing the same thing. If you keep doing the same wrong thing, people will assume that you really are not sorry.

Think about Frank, and decide if you think he was really sorry.

Frank's little brother Ryan was really a pest. Ryan would take Frank's comic books and then wouldn't return them.

Frank felt that his parents always took his brother's side. They would say, "Ryan is your younger brother, and he doesn't understand as much as you do. You just have to put up with him."

One day, Ryan was being so annoying that Frank threw the remote control at him and hit Ryan on his head. Ryan cried and cried, and by that evening he had a big bruise on his forehead.

Frank's mother said, "Do you know that you could have hit your brother in the eye and really done some damage? Ryan could be blind in that eye, and it would all be because you couldn't control your temper. Is that what you want?"

"No," Frank said. "That's not what I want."

"Then what do you say to your younger brother?" Frank's mom asked.

"I'm sorry," said Frank to Ryan.

"That's all?" his mother asked.

"I'm very sorry," Frank said.

Saying you're sorry is not enough when you have done something wrong to someone else, particularly if you have hurt them. This activity will help you think about ways to apologize that show you are sincere.

In the space below, write a letter to someone you owe an apology to for something you did in anger.

Dear _____,

I'm really sorry that I _____
_____.

I know that _____
_____.

It is wrong _____
_____.

The next time _____
_____.

To show you how sorry I am, I would like to _____
_____
_____.

Sincerely,

_____

... And More to Do

Read the story about Frank and his brother Ryan again. What do you think Frank could have done to show his parents that he was sorry?

_____

_____

Do you think that Frank owed his brother an apology? What should he have said or done?

_____

_____

Have you ever hurt someone in anger, even though you didn't mean to? What happened?

_____

_____

Have you ever hurt someone's feelings in anger? How can you make someone feel better if you have hurt their feelings?

_____

_____

_____

For You to Know

Being a good sport can be hard. You might feel angry or jealous or be disappointed in yourself about something that has happened. Even so, you can still act in ways that show you can control your feelings and do the right thing.

Do you know what being a "good sport" means? It means being pleasant and considerate of others, even if you are not happy about what happened. If you lose at a game, you can be a good sport by congratulating the winner. If you know someone who got a good mark on a test, you can say something nice to that person, even if you didn't do well and feel bad for yourself.

Being a good sport is important to keeping your friends, because it is hard to be friends with a bad sport. Being a good sport often requires you to understand that everyone is different and that some people may be better than you at some things.

Consider this story of the rabbit and the turtle. (It may be different from the one you usually hear.)

Once upon a time, a turtle and a rabbit were very good friends. They liked to sleep over at each other's houses, make popcorn, and stay up late watching scary movies (when their parents would let them, of course). They liked to read books to each other. They liked to play games like checkers and Parcheesi.

But they didn't like to play sports together. The rabbit, as you might expect, was very fast, and the turtle, as you might expect, was very slow. The rabbit was great at baseball and basketball and football. And, of course, he always won when there was a race. The turtle never enjoyed any sport because he was so slow and clumsy. Because the rabbit loved to play sports and the turtle didn't, they found that they were spending less and less time together and that they were not as good friends as they used to be.

The rabbit thought to himself: "If only my friend the turtle would try a little harder, then he would enjoy the sports I like."

The turtle thought to himself: "If only my friend the rabbit would not play sports all the time, then we could do more fun things together."

But neither the rabbit nor the turtle told the other what he was thinking.

Then one day as they were walking down the street, the rabbit passed a sign that said, "Bowling Is for Everyone! Bowl Now at Harry's Bowling Alley."

"Do you bowl?" the rabbit asked his friend.

"Why, yes, I like bowling," said the turtle. "Do you bowl?" he asked the rabbit.

Yes, I do," said the rabbit. "I love to bowl. Why don't we go bowl a game right now?"

And so they bowled all afternoon. And the turtle won every game they played.

The Moral of the Story: Everyone has different likes and dislikes and different strengths and weaknesses. But if you are a good sport and treat other people with respect, you will get your turn to shine, and you will have strong friendships.

Imagine you received a trophy for being a good sport. Color it, and then write what you did to deserve this trophy.

_____

_____

_____

_____

_____

... And More to Do

What is your favorite sport? Have you ever seen someone be a sore loser at this sport? Tell what happened to this person as a result.

_____

_____

_____

_____

What is something you like to do, even though you know that you are not very good at it? Explain why you like doing this thing.

_____

_____

_____

_____

Have you ever been polite and kind to someone even though you didn't feel like it? How did you control your feelings?

_____

_____

_____

_____

For You to Know

Lots of kids live in homes where there is a lot of yelling and arguing. Sometimes brothers and sisters argue with each other; sometimes parents argue with each other; sometimes everybody argues. Families can learn to solve their problems through family meetings.

Some families seem to get along very well. But in other families, there are lots of disagreements. This is a problem for kids, especially when parents are involved, because no child likes to hear their parents argue.

Most children don't know what to do when their parents fight. Some children hide in their rooms. Some children try to spend as much time as possible away from home. Other children yell at their parents when they fight.

But there is really only one thing that you can do when your parents fight: tell them how it makes you feel. If your parents fight when you are around, you can say:

I feel (fill in the right word) when you fight in front of me, particularly when you (describe the thing that really bothers you). I wish you wouldn't argue in front of me.

There are many people who can help parents who fight and argue, including counselors and religious leaders and even relatives. But it is up to your parents to get help. It is also up to you to find someone to talk to if you need help with this problem.

It takes some time for families to learn that they will be happier when they work together, but family meetings can also help. Your family can get together and try to solve a problem or make a decision that will benefit everyone. Families have meetings to think about ways they can get along better, to make up a schedule, to plan a vacation, to divide up chores, and for many other reasons. You don't even have to have a problem to have a family meeting. You can use the meeting to talk about things that happened during the week, and just to have fun together!

In this activity, you will create an agenda, which is a plan for what you would like to talk about. Having an agenda for family meetings is a good way to make sure that important things aren't forgotten. You can fill in the agenda yourself, but parents usually plan and lead family meetings, so it will be best if they help you.

The Agenda for Your Family Meeting

Write down one important problem you want to discuss.

_____

_____

_____

Write down two or three things that you think your family needs to plan (for example, a birthday celebration, a trip, or what to do on the weekend).

_____

_____

_____

Write down three questions each family member can answer to help them share their thoughts and feelings, for example, "What was the best thing that happened to you this week?" "What is something you are really looking forward to?" "What are some things we can do together for fun?"

_____

_____

_____

A Workbook to Help Kids Control Their Anger

... And More to Do

Have you ever had a family meeting? What happened?

_____

_____

_____

Why do you think it is important to have family meetings?

_____

_____

Can you think of something you would not like to discuss at a family meeting because it is private?

_____

_____

Do you know any families where everyone seems to get along really well? Is there anything about these families that your family should imitate?

_____

_____

_____

_____

For You to Know

Being a cooperative person will help you be appreciated by kids and adults. When you have a cooperative attitude, you look for ways to help other people, both kids and adults.

Would you call yourself a cooperative person? The following statements describe someone who is cooperative. Check off the ones that describe you:

☐ When my mom or dad asks me to do something, I do it right away.

☐ I like to help other people.

☐ I never argue with other kids when we do projects at school.

☐ I help my teacher whenever I can.

☐ I listen carefully when someone is speaking to me.

☐ I don't mind sharing my things with other kids, even my brother or sister.

☐ I take turns without complaining.

☐ I like doing group projects.

☐ I like to include other kids, even ones I don't know, in my activities.

☐ I think it is more fun to work with other kids than to work by myself.

If you checked off more than seven of these statements, you are a cooperative kid. If you checked off all ten, you are a very cooperative kid. But if you checked no more than five, you need to think about the importance of being more cooperative and to work on this behavior.

This maze will help you see why it is important to be cooperative. The questions that follow it will help you think about times and ways that you can be more cooperative. The maze is pretty simple and yet it is also hard. Why? Because you will have to do it blindfolded!

Ask an adult or another child to help you with this activity. Tie a bandana or cloth around your head so that it covers your eyes. Ask your partner to guide your hand so that your pencil is at the start of the maze. Now your partner will have to tell you which way to move to complete the maze: right, left, up, or down.

If you cross the lines fewer than five times, you and your partner get a prize. Can you cooperate and pick out a prize or reward that will please you both?

Cooperation Maze

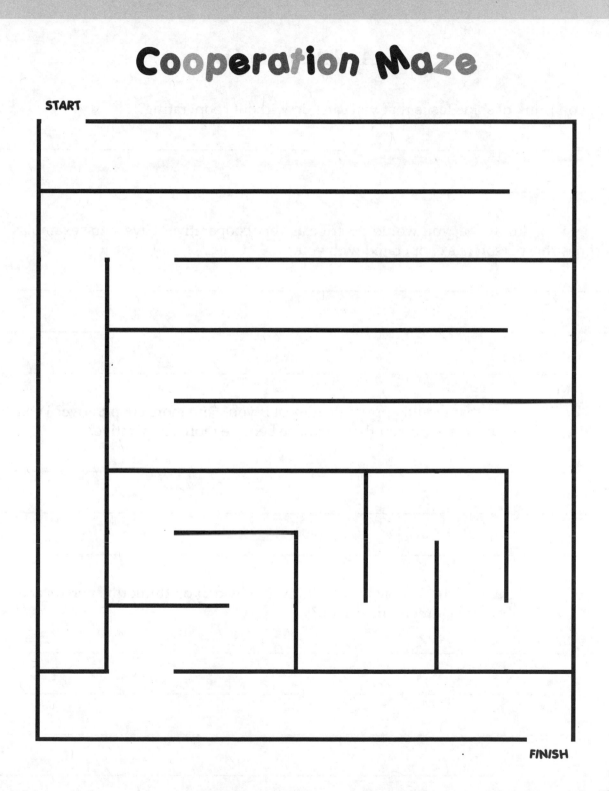

... *And More to Do*

Can you think of some tasks that you can't do without cooperating?

_____

_____

Who do you know that you would describe as very cooperative? Give some examples of times this person has cooperated with you.

_____

_____

_____

Who do you know that would appreciate it most if you were more cooperative? What could you do to show this person that you have become more cooperative?

_____

_____

_____

Do you know anyone who is very uncooperative? Why do you think this person acts this way? What would change this person?

_____

_____

_____

_____

For You to Know

There are lots of times when we blame others for our problems, even though our own behavior caused or contributed to the problem. Blaming others never helps, and it usually makes things worse.

Two-year-old Bea fell and hit her head on the coffee table. She cried and cried, and a big lump swelled on her forehead. When she stopped crying, she said, "Bad table," and she kicked the table as hard as she could. Her mom smiled and agreed, saying, "Bad coffee table! Why did you trip my little girl?"

We know, just as Bea's mom did, that it wasn't the table's fault at all, but when you are little, you tend to blame other people or other things for your problems. When you get older, your first reaction may still be to blame something or someone else for your problems, but once you think about it, you start to take responsibility for what happened to you. If you don't take responsibility, you will likely stay mad and even repeat the problem. Consider the following situations:

- Sam hardly studied at all for his math test, and he got a D minus. He told his mother, "My teacher didn't explain the math, so that's why I did badly."

- Tanya bragged constantly about all the things she had and all the things she could do. At first, the other girls in her class tried to ignore her bragging, but after a while they just avoided her. One day Tanya found out that all the girls in her class had been invited to Miriam's bowling party, except for her. Tanya told her mother, "Miriam is really mean. I hate her."

- Mr. Wainright was driving too fast down the highway, talking on the cell phone, and eating a sandwich. When the driver in front of him braked suddenly, Mr. Wainright crashed right into his car. "What an idiot!" Mr. Wainright shouted. "I can't believe the way that guy was driving."

Sam, Tanya, and Mr. Wainwright are all letting the Blame Monster take over. Do you know the Blame Monster? It lives inside all of us, waiting for an opportunity to blame someone else for our problems. In the space below, draw a picture of your Blame Monster.

Now make this box into a cage! Draw in the bars, and put on a good lock. See if you can take responsibility for your problems and keep your Blame Monster locked up.

... And More to Do

Have you ever been blamed for something you didn't do? Describe what happened.

_____

_____

_____

Have you ever blamed one of your parents for a problem that you caused? What happened?

_____

_____

_____

Why do you think people don't want to admit that they caused their own problems?

_____

_____

Being responsible shows good character. Can you think of three ways that you are a responsible kid?

_____

_____

_____

For You to Know

If you can change things that are going wrong in your life, you may be less angry. But there are some problems you can do nothing about. You will have to learn to cope with those situations the best you can. Trying to change them will just make you more angry.

Ashleigh was mad at Marcie because Marcie ignored her on the playground. Instead of getting angry, Ashleigh found someone else to play with. This is an example of avoiding the things that are bothering you. In Activity 4, you learned about identifying your anger buttons and how you can avoid having your buttons pushed.

There are other things you can do about situations that make you angry. In Activity 18, you learned about problem solving. In Activity 25, you learned how to think about a situation differently by seeing it from another person's point of view. In Activity 30, you learned about making compromises.

Here are some things that get kids upset but can't be changed:

- Heather is mad because her parents are getting a divorce.

- Katie is mad because her parents are having a new baby and she thinks they are too old to have more kids.

- Michael is mad because his family is moving to another state and he will have to quit his basketball team and leave his friends.

- Jack is mad because he hates doing homework.

On the chart on the next page, write down ten things that make you angry. They can be little things or big things. Then put a check mark in the next column if you think you can change this situation. You can write in how you can change it now, or you can come back to this activity after you have finished this book. Put an X in the next column if you can't change the situation.

The next few activities will teach you how to cope with things you can't change. After you have completed them, you can fill in the last column.

Situations That Make You Angry	Situations You Can Change	What You Can Do to Change This Situation	Situations You Can't Change	What You Can Do to Cope with This Situation

... And More to Do

Reread your list. Which are the three situations that make you the most angry?

_____

_____

_____

Which are the three that bother you the least?

_____

_____

_____

Look at the situations you thought you couldn't change. Is there a way to change each a little? What can you do?

_____

_____

_____

How do you feel after doing this activity? Does it make you angry to think that there are situations you can't change? Does it make you feel better to understand what you can change and what you can't?

_____

_____

_____

I'm Not Bad, I'm Just Mad

For You to Know

Humor helps just about any difficult situation. Humor can give you a different perspective on your problems and it can lighten your mood. Having a sense of humor about your problems will keep you from getting angry.

Did you know that humor can help you get better when you are sick? Scientists tell us that laughing helps our bodies fight almost every illness. Some hospitals even have clowns who visit and make people laugh.

Humor also helps us with difficult feelings. Even when you are really, really angry, you can learn to laugh. When you laugh, the thing that was making you so mad will probably not seem so important.

Humor is also important in making friends. Kids like other kids who are funny, and even more, they like kids who can laugh.

Do you laugh a lot? If not, try the following:

- Make faces in the mirror.

- Get a joke book from the library and learn a new joke every day.

- Ask a parent or a friend to pick out a funny movie to watch with you.

- Tickle your feet with a feather.

- Ask a friend to tell you a joke or funny story.

There are lots of ways to bring more laughter into every day. We guarantee that this will help you feel better about yourself and others. One of the things that almost always gets us laughing is when something ordinary is combined with something unusual.

There are four ordinary kids shown below. Add something to each picture to make it funny.

I'm Not Bad, I'm Just Mad

... And More to Do

Who is the funniest person you know?

_____

_____

_____

What is your favorite comedy on television?

_____

What is a funny movie that you'd like your parents to watch with you?

_____

What other kid do you think is funny? What makes this kid so funny?

_____

_____

_____

_____

For You to Know

Holding on to anger doesn't do anyone any good. It is better to just forgive and forget.

Some people hold on to their anger for a very long time. Sometimes you can be angry at someone for such a long time that you forget what you are angry about! But holding on to your anger won't make you feel better, and it certainly won't help you in your relationships.

Forgiveness can be hard for some people. They seem to prefer staying angry, even though they know it is not helpful. Other people might like to forgive, but don't know how.

Take Emily, for example. She was mad at Tyra for not inviting her to her birthday party. Emily never knew why she wasn't invited, and she never asked. But she stopped talking to Tyra and even turned away when Tyra passed by at school. Months went by and Emily still wouldn't talk to Tyra. Tyra didn't know what was wrong, because Emily had never told her. The two girls had been good friends before, but now it was as if they were enemies.

Then it was time for Emily's birthday party. She made up a list of kids to invite and she wrote Tyra's name down without even thinking. When she remembered that she was mad at Tyra, she still didn't cross Tyra's name out. She missed talking with Tyra and she wanted to invite her to her party. So she did.

Tyra came to the party and gave Emily a wonderful present and a card she had made. The card said, "Let's be friends again."

Sometimes the best way to forgive and forget is to reach out to someone you have been mad at, as if nothing wrong had ever happened. That person may respond positively, or they may not. You never know exactly what people will do. But you can count on feeling better about yourself when you are forgiving. Once you forgive, it is easy to forget what you were upset about. It simply won't be important anymore.

In the picture of the heart below, write in anything you are mad about. You can write in several things if you like. Now color in the heart with a red crayon or marker. Color it in so fully that you can no longer see the things you are mad at.

... *And More to Do*

Who is a person famous for being forgiving?

_____

Can you think of something that you did wrong and were forgiven for?

_____

_____

Why do you think it is hard for some people to be forgiving?

_____

_____

_____

Can you think of someone you need to forgive?

_____

For You to Know

If you are really serious about controlling your anger, then you should sign a contract that says you will try as hard as you can.

A contract between two people is an agreement to do something that benefits both of them. When people rent an apartment or buy a house, they sign a contract. When people buy a cell phone, they sign a contract that says they will pay a cell phone company a certain amount of money each month. Contracts are very important in the adult world. When someone signs a contract, it means they promise to do something, and if they don't do what they promise, there will be a problem.

Contracts that kids sign are called behavioral contracts. When kids sign them, they promise that they will behave in a certain way. Usually adults help kids change their behavior by giving them a special reward when the kids do what the contract says. That way, both the kids and the adults are happy. Special rewards can be privileges, like spending more time on the computer, or special treats, like going to a baseball game or a concert, or something that you want for yourself, like getting a DVD or a video game.

On the next page is a contract for you to sign when you are ready to control your anger.

Sign the contract below when you are ready to control your anger. Ask your parents or another adult if they will agree to give you a reward for changing your behavior. They should sign this contract too.

I, _____, promise to control my anger better.

I will not _____.

I will _____.

If I keep my promise for one month, I will get _____.

Signed,

Your name _____

Adult's name _____

... And More to Do

Why do you think it is important to control your anger?

_____

_____

Even though you have made a promise and signed a contract to control your anger, things may happen that make it hard for you to keep your promise. What do you think might happen that will make it hard for you to keep your promise?

_____

_____

_____

What can you do if you find yourself going back to your old anger habits?

_____

_____

What is one thing you learned in this book that will really help if you start to get mad about something?

_____

_____

_____

Lawrence E. Shapiro, Ph.D., is a nationally recognized child psychologist and parenting expert. He has written dozens of books to help children learn the emotional intelligence skills that make them happier, healthier, and more successful.

Zach Pelta-Heller holds an MFA in non-fiction from The New School. He is a freelance writer whose work has appeared in The Huffington Post, American Prospect, and Alternet, among other publications. Currently, he lives in Philadelphia with his wife, Anna.

Anna F. Greenwald is currently pursuing her MSS at the Bryn Mawr Graduate School of Social Work and Social Research. She was previously a preschool teacher, and now resides in Philadelphia with her husband.

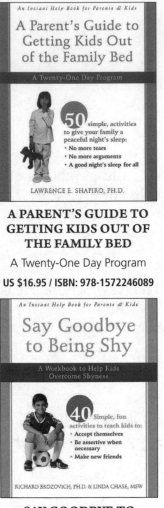